Seemeilen-Nachweis
Confirmation of nautical miles

AF209995

Seemeilen-Nachweis
Confirmation of nautical miles

Bibliografische Information der Deutschen
Nationalbibliothek
Die Deutsche Nationalbibliothek verzeichnet diese
Publikation in der Deutschen Nationalbibliografie;
detailliertere bibliografische Daten sind im Internet
über http://dnd.d-nb.de abrufbar.

Herstellung und Verlag: Books on Demand GmbH,
Norderstedt
978-3837092158

Inhalt / Index

Foto
Photo

Name Name	_____
Geburtstag Date of birth	_____
Geburtsort Place of birth	_____
Unterschrift Signature	_____
Straße Street	_____
PLZ und Ort ZIP Code, City	_____
Land Country	_____

Bei Anschriftwechsel / If address changes, please update accordingly

Straße Street	_____
PLZ und Ort ZIP Code, City	_____
Land Country	_____

Führerscheine
Licenses Held

Führerschein License	Datum Date	Nummer Number

Andere Zertifikate (z.B. Funk)
Other certificates (e.g. radio)

Zertifikat Certificate	Datum Date	Nummer Number

Übersicht Törns
Trip Summary

Nr. No.	Gebiet Area	Datum Date	Meilen Miles
Übertrag aus anderen Nachweisen Carryover from other confirmations			
1.			
2.			
3.			
4.			
5.			
6.			
7.			
8.			
9.			
10.			
11.			
12.			
13.			
14.			
15.			
Summe Total			

Übersicht Törns
Trip Summary

Nr. No.	Gebiet Area	Datum Date	Meilen Miles
Übertrag aus der ersten Seite Carryover from the first page			
16.			
17.			
18.			
19.			
20.			
21.			
22.			
23.			
24.			
25.			
26.			
27.			
28.			
29.			
30.			
Summe Total			

Crew:

_____

_____

_____

_____

_____

_____

Sonstiges / Miscellaneous

Nr. 1 / No. 1

Schiffsname
Name of vessel
_____

Schiffsmodell
Model of vessel
_____

□ Segel / sailing Yacht   □ Tide / tidal waters
□ Motor / power Yacht   □ keine Tide / non-tidal waters

Eigner
Owner
_____

Flagge
Flag
_____

Reisedatum
Date of trip
_____

Fahrtgebiet
Area of trip
_____

Reiseroute
Route of trip
_____

_____

Anzahl der Seemeilen
Number of nautical miles
_____

Funktion auf dem Schiff
Position on board
_____

Angaben zum Schiffsführer / personal data of the skipper:

Name
Name
_____

Straße
Street
_____

Plz und Ort
ZIP Code, City
_____

Land
Country
_____

Lizenz des Skippers
License of skipper
_____

Ort, Datum
Location, date
_____

Unterschrift Skipper
Signature of skipper
_____

Nr. 2 / No. 2
Kommentare / Comments

Crew:

_____

_____

_____

_____

_____

_____

Sonstiges / Miscellaneous

Schiffsname
Name of vessel
_____

Schiffsmodell
Model of vessel
_____

☐ Segel / sailing Yacht   ☐ Tide / tidal waters
☐ Motor / power Yacht   ☐ keine Tide / non-tidal waters

Eigner
Owner
_____

Flagge
Flag
_____

Reisedatum
Date of trip
_____

Fahrtgebiet
Area of trip
_____

Reiseroute
Route of trip
_____

_____

Anzahl der Seemeilen
Number of nautical miles
_____

Funktion auf dem Schiff
Position on board
_____

Angaben zum Schiffsführer / personal data of the skipper:

Name
Name
_____

Straße
Street
_____

Plz und Ort
ZIP Code, City
_____

Land
Country
_____

Lizenz des Skippers
License of skipper
_____

Ort, Datum
Location, date
_____

Unterschrift Skipper
Signature skipper
_____

Nr. 3 / No. 3
Kommentare / Comments

Crew:

_____

_____

_____

_____

_____

_____

Sonstiges / Miscellaneous

Schiffsname
Name of vessel
_____

Schiffsmodell
Model of vessel
_____

☐ Segel / sailing Yacht   ☐ Tide / tidal waters
☐ Motor / power Yacht   ☐ keine Tide / non-tidal waters

Eigner
Owner
_____

Flagge
Flag
_____

Reisedatum
Date of trip
_____

Fahrtgebiet
Area of trip
_____

Reiseroute
Route of trip
_____

_____

Anzahl der Seemeilen
Number of nautical miles
_____

Funktion auf dem Schiff
Position on board
_____

Angaben zum Schiffsführer / personal data of the skipper:

Name
Name
_____

Straße
Street
_____

Plz und Ort
ZIP Code, City
_____

Land
Country
_____

Lizenz des Skippers
License of skipper
_____

Ort, Datum
Location, date
_____

Unterschrift Skipper
Signature skipper
_____

Nr. 4 / No. 4
Kommentare / Comments

Crew:

_____

_____

_____

_____

_____

_____

Sonstiges / Miscellaneous

Nr. 4 / No. 4

Schiffsname
Name of vessel
_____

Schiffsmodell
Model of vessel
_____

☐ Segel / sailing Yacht   ☐ Tide / tidal waters
☐ Motor / power Yacht   ☐ keine Tide / non-tidal waters

Eigner
Owner
_____

Flagge
Flag
_____

Reisedatum
Date of trip
_____

Fahrtgebiet
Area of trip
_____

Reiseroute
Route of trip
_____

_____

Anzahl der Seemeilen
Number of nautical miles
_____

Funktion auf dem Schiff
Position on board
_____

Angaben zum Schiffsführer / personal data of the skipper:

Name
Name
_____

Straße
Street
_____

Plz und Ort
ZIP Code, City
_____

Land
Country
_____

Lizenz des Skippers
License of skipper
_____

Ort, Datum
Location, date
_____

Unterschrift Skipper
Signature skipper
_____

Nr. 5 / No. 5
Kommentare / Comments

Crew:

_____

_____

_____

_____

_____

_____

Sonstiges / Miscellaneous

Schiffsname
Name of vessel   _____

Schiffsmodell
Model of vessel   _____

☐ Segel / sailing Yacht   ☐ Tide / tidal waters
☐ Motor / power Yacht   ☐ keine Tide / non-tidal waters

Eigner
Owner   _____

Flagge
Flag   _____

Reisedatum
Date of trip   _____

Fahrtgebiet
Area of trip   _____

Reiseroute
Route of trip   _____

                                        _____

Anzahl der Seemeilen
Number of nautical miles   _____

Funktion auf dem Schiff
Position on board   _____

Angaben zum Schiffsführer / personal data of the skipper:

Name
Name   _____

Straße
Street   _____

Plz und Ort
ZIP Code, City   _____

Land
Country   _____

Lizenz des Skippers
License of skipper   _____

Ort, Datum
Location, date   _____

Unterschrift Skipper
Signature skipper   _____

Nr. 6 / No. 6
Kommentare / Comments

Crew:

_____

_____

_____

_____

_____

_____

Sonstiges / Miscellaneous

Schiffsname
Name of vessel
_____

Schiffsmodell
Model of vessel
_____

☐ Segel / sailing Yacht   ☐ Tide / tidal waters
☐ Motor / power Yacht   ☐ keine Tide / non-tidal waters

Eigner
Owner
_____

Flagge
Flag
_____

Reisedatum
Date of trip
_____

Fahrtgebiet
Area of trip
_____

Reiseroute
Route of trip
_____

_____

Anzahl der Seemeilen
Number of nautical miles
_____

Funktion auf dem Schiff
Position on board
_____

Angaben zum Schiffsführer / personal data of the skipper:

Name
Name
_____

Straße
Street
_____

Plz und Ort
ZIP Code, City
_____

Land
Country
_____

Lizenz des Skippers
License of skipper
_____

Ort, Datum
Location, date
_____

Unterschrift Skipper
Signature skipper
_____

Nr. 7 / No. 7
Kommentare / Comments

Crew:

_____

_____

_____

_____

_____

_____

Sonstiges / Miscellaneous

Schiffsname
Name of vessel
_____

Schiffsmodell
Model of vessel
_____

☐ Segel / sailing Yacht   ☐ Tide / tidal waters
☐ Motor / power Yacht   ☐ keine Tide / non-tidal waters

Eigner
Owner
_____

Flagge
Flag
_____

Reisedatum
Date of trip
_____

Fahrtgebiet
Area of trip
_____

Reiseroute
Route of trip
_____

_____

Anzahl der Seemeilen
Number of nautical miles
_____

Funktion auf dem Schiff
Position on board
_____

Angaben zum Schiffsführer / personal data of the skipper:

Name
Name
_____

Straße
Street
_____

Plz und Ort
ZIP Code, City
_____

Land
Country
_____

Lizenz des Skippers
License of skipper
_____

Ort, Datum
Location, date
_____

Unterschrift Skipper
Signature skipper
_____

Nr. 8 / No. 8
Kommentare / Comments

Crew:

_____

_____

_____

_____

_____

_____

Sonstiges / Miscellaneous

Schiffsname
Name of vessel _____

Schiffsmodell
Model of vessel _____

☐ Segel / sailing Yacht   ☐ Tide / tidal waters
☐ Motor / power Yacht   ☐ keine Tide / non-tidal waters

Eigner
Owner _____

Flagge
Flag _____

Reisedatum
Date of trip _____

Fahrtgebiet
Area of trip _____

Reiseroute
Route of trip _____

_____

Anzahl der Seemeilen
Number of nautical miles _____

Funktion auf dem Schiff
Position on board _____

Angaben zum Schiffsführer / personal data of the skipper:

Name
Name _____

Straße
Street _____

Plz und Ort
ZIP Code, City _____

Land
Country _____

Lizenz des Skippers
License of skipper _____

Ort, Datum
Location, date _____

Unterschrift Skipper
Signature skipper _____

Nr. 9 / No. 9
Kommentare / Comments

Crew:

_____

_____

_____

_____

_____

_____

Sonstiges / Miscellaneous

Schiffsname
Name of vessel
_____

Schiffsmodell
Model of vessel
_____

☐ Segel / sailing Yacht   ☐ Tide / tidal waters
☐ Motor / power Yacht   ☐ keine Tide / non-tidal waters

Eigner
Owner
_____

Flagge
Flag
_____

Reisedatum
Date of trip
_____

Fahrtgebiet
Area of trip
_____

Reiseroute
Route of trip
_____

_____

Anzahl der Seemeilen
Number of nautical miles
_____

Funktion auf dem Schiff
Position on board
_____

Angaben zum Schiffsführer / personal data of the skipper:

Name
Name
_____

Straße
Street
_____

Plz und Ort
ZIP Code, City
_____

Land
Country
_____

Lizenz des Skippers
License of skipper
_____

Ort, Datum
Location, date
_____

Unterschrift Skipper
Signature skipper
_____

Nr. 10 / No. 10
Kommentare / Comments

Crew:

_____

_____

_____

_____

_____

_____

Sonstiges / Miscellaneous

Schiffsname
Name of vessel

_____

Schiffsmodell
Model of vessel

_____

☐ Segel / sailing Yacht   ☐ Tide / tidal waters
☐ Motor / power Yacht   ☐ keine Tide / non-tidal waters

Eigner
Owner

_____

Flagge
Flag

_____

Reisedatum
Date of trip

_____

Fahrtgebiet
Area of trip

_____

Reiseroute
Route of trip

_____

_____

Anzahl der Seemeilen
Number of nautical miles

_____

Funktion auf dem Schiff
Position on board

_____

Angaben zum Schiffsführer / personal data of the skipper:

Name
Name

_____

Straße
Street

_____

Plz und Ort
ZIP Code, City

_____

Land
Country

_____

Lizenz des Skippers
License of skipper

_____

Ort, Datum
Location, date

_____

Unterschrift Skipper
Signature skipper

_____

Crew:

_____

_____

_____

_____

_____

_____

Sonstiges / Miscellaneous

Schiffsname
Name of vessel
_____

Schiffsmodell
Model of vessel
_____

☐ Segel / sailing Yacht   ☐ Tide / tidal waters
☐ Motor / power Yacht   ☐ keine Tide / non-tidal waters

Eigner
Owner
_____

Flagge
Flag
_____

Reisedatum
Date of trip
_____

Fahrtgebiet
Area of trip
_____

Reiseroute
Route of trip
_____

_____

Anzahl der Seemeilen
Number of nautical miles
_____

Funktion auf dem Schiff
Position on board
_____

Angaben zum Schiffsführer / personal data of the skipper:

Name
Name
_____

Straße
Street
_____

Plz und Ort
ZIP Code, City
_____

Land
Country
_____

Lizenz des Skippers
License of skipper
_____

Ort, Datum
Location, date
_____

Unterschrift Skipper
Signature skipper
_____

Nr. 12 / No. 12
Kommentare / Comments

Crew:

_____

_____

_____

_____

_____

_____

Sonstiges / Miscellaneous

Nr. 12 / No. 12

Schiffsname
Name of vessel
_____

Schiffsmodell
Model of vessel
_____

☐ Segel / sailing Yacht ☐ Tide / tidal waters
☐ Motor / power Yacht ☐ keine Tide / non-tidal waters

Eigner
Owner
_____

Flagge
Flag
_____

Reisedatum
Date of trip
_____

Fahrtgebiet
Area of trip
_____

Reiseroute
Route of trip
_____

_____

Anzahl der Seemeilen
Number of nautical miles
_____

Funktion auf dem Schiff
Position on board
_____

Angaben zum Schiffsführer / personal data of the skipper:

Name
Name
_____

Straße
Street
_____

Plz und Ort
ZIP Code, City
_____

Land
Country
_____

Lizenz des Skippers
License of skipper
_____

Ort, Datum
Location, date
_____

Unterschrift Skipper
Signature skipper
_____

Crew:

_____

_____

_____

_____

_____

_____

Sonstiges / Miscellaneous

Nr. 13 / No. 13

Schiffsname
Name of vessel
_____

Schiffsmodell
Model of vessel
_____

☐ Segel / sailing Yacht   ☐ Tide / tidal waters
☐ Motor / power Yacht   ☐ keine Tide / non-tidal waters

Eigner
Owner
_____

Flagge
Flag
_____

Reisedatum
Date of trip
_____

Fahrtgebiet
Area of trip
_____

Reiseroute
Route of trip
_____

_____

Anzahl der Seemeilen
Number of nautical miles
_____

Funktion auf dem Schiff
Position on board
_____

Angaben zum Schiffsführer / personal data of the skipper:

Name
Name
_____

Straße
Street
_____

Plz und Ort
ZIP Code, City
_____

Land
Country
_____

Lizenz des Skippers
License of skipper
_____

Ort, Datum
Location, date
_____

Unterschrift Skipper
Signature skipper
_____

Crew:

_____

_____

_____

_____

_____

_____

Sonstiges / Miscellaneous

Schiffsname
Name of vessel
_____

Schiffsmodell
Model of vessel
_____

☐ Segel / sailing Yacht   ☐ Tide / tidal waters
☐ Motor / power Yacht   ☐ keine Tide / non-tidal waters

Eigner
Owner
_____

Flagge
Flag
_____

Reisedatum
Date of trip
_____

Fahrtgebiet
Area of trip
_____

Reiseroute
Route of trip
_____

_____

Anzahl der Seemeilen
Number of nautical miles
_____

Funktion auf dem Schiff
Position on board
_____

Angaben zum Schiffsführer / personal data of the skipper:

Name
Name
_____

Straße
Street
_____

Plz und Ort
ZIP Code, City
_____

Land
Country
_____

Lizenz des Skippers
License of skipper
_____

Ort, Datum
Location, date
_____

Unterschrift Skipper
Signature skipper
_____

Crew:

_____

_____

_____

_____

_____

_____

Sonstiges / Miscellaneous

Nr. 15 / No. 15

Schiffsname
Name of vessel
_____

Schiffsmodell
Model of vessel
_____

☐ Segel / sailing Yacht   ☐ Tide / tidal waters
☐ Motor / power Yacht   ☐ keine Tide / non-tidal waters

Eigner
Owner
_____

Flagge
Flag
_____

Reisedatum
Date of trip
_____

Fahrtgebiet
Area of trip
_____

Reiseroute
Route of trip
_____

_____

Anzahl der Seemeilen
Number of nautical miles
_____

Funktion auf dem Schiff
Position on board
_____

Angaben zum Schiffsführer / personal data of the skipper:

Name
Name
_____

Straße
Street
_____

Plz und Ort
ZIP Code, City
_____

Land
Country
_____

Lizenz des Skippers
License of skipper
_____

Ort, Datum
Location, date
_____

Unterschrift Skipper
Signature skipper
_____

Crew:

_____

_____

_____

_____

_____

_____

Sonstiges / Miscellaneous

Nr. 16 / No. 16

Schiffsname
Name of vessel
_____

Schiffsmodell
Model of vessel
_____

☐ Segel / sailing Yacht   ☐ Tide / tidal waters
☐ Motor / power Yacht   ☐ keine Tide / non-tidal waters

Eigner
Owner
_____

Flagge
Flag
_____

Reisedatum
Date of trip
_____

Fahrtgebiet
Area of trip
_____

Reiseroute
Route of trip
_____

_____

Anzahl der Seemeilen
Number of nautical miles
_____

Funktion auf dem Schiff
Position on board
_____

Angaben zum Schiffsführer / personal data of the skipper:

Name
Name
_____

Straße
Street
_____

Plz und Ort
ZIP Code, City
_____

Land
Country
_____

Lizenz des Skippers
License of skipper
_____

Ort, Datum
Location, date
_____

Unterschrift Skipper
Signature skipper
_____

Nr. 17 / No. 17
Kommentare / Comments

Crew:

_____

_____

_____

_____

_____

_____

Sonstiges / Miscellaneous

Schiffsname
Name of vessel
_____

Schiffsmodell
Model of vessel
_____

☐ Segel / sailing Yacht   ☐ Tide / tidal waters
☐ Motor / power Yacht   ☐ keine Tide / non-tidal waters

Eigner
Owner
_____

Flagge
Flag
_____

Reisedatum
Date of trip
_____

Fahrtgebiet
Area of trip
_____

Reiseroute
Route of trip
_____

_____

Anzahl der Seemeilen
Number of nautical miles
_____

Funktion auf dem Schiff
Position on board
_____

Angaben zum Schiffsführer / personal data of the skipper:

Name
Name
_____

Straße
Street
_____

Plz und Ort
ZIP Code, City
_____

Land
Country
_____

Lizenz des Skippers
License of skipper
_____

Ort, Datum
Location, date
_____

Unterschrift Skipper
Signature skipper
_____

Crew:

_____

_____

_____

_____

_____

_____

Sonstiges / Miscellaneous

Schiffsname
Name of vessel
_____

Schiffsmodell
Model of vessel
_____

☐ Segel / sailing Yacht   ☐ Tide / tidal waters
☐ Motor / power Yacht   ☐ keine Tide / non-tidal waters

Eigner
Owner
_____

Flagge
Flag
_____

Reisedatum
Date of trip
_____

Fahrtgebiet
Area of trip
_____

Reiseroute
Route of trip
_____

_____

Anzahl der Seemeilen
Number of nautical miles
_____

Funktion auf dem Schiff
Position on board
_____

Angaben zum Schiffsführer / personal data of the skipper:

Name
Name
_____

Straße
Street
_____

Plz und Ort
ZIP Code, City
_____

Land
Country
_____

Lizenz des Skippers
License of skipper
_____

Ort, Datum
Location, date
_____

Unterschrift Skipper
Signature skipper
_____

Nr. 19 / No. 19
Kommentare / Comments

Crew:

_____

_____

_____

_____

_____

_____

Sonstiges / Miscellaneous

Schiffsname
Name of vessel
_____

Schiffsmodell
Model of vessel
_____

☐ Segel / sailing Yacht   ☐ Tide / tidal waters
☐ Motor / power Yacht   ☐ keine Tide / non-tidal waters

Eigner
Owner
_____

Flagge
Flag
_____

Reisedatum
Date of trip
_____

Fahrtgebiet
Area of trip
_____

Reiseroute
Route of trip
_____

_____

Anzahl der Seemeilen
Number of nautical miles
_____

Funktion auf dem Schiff
Position on board
_____

Angaben zum Schiffsführer / personal data of the skipper:

Name
Name
_____

Straße
Street
_____

Plz und Ort
ZIP Code, City
_____

Land
Country
_____

Lizenz des Skippers
License of skipper
_____

Ort, Datum
Location, date
_____

Unterschrift Skipper
Signature skipper
_____

Nr. 20 / No. 20
Kommentare / Comments

Crew:

_____

_____

_____

_____

_____

_____

Sonstiges / Miscellaneous

Nr. 20 / No. 20

Schiffsname
Name of vessel
_____

Schiffsmodell
Model of vessel
_____

☐ Segel / sailing Yacht   ☐ Tide / tidal waters
☐ Motor / power Yacht   ☐ keine Tide / non-tidal waters

Eigner
Owner
_____

Flagge
Flag
_____

Reisedatum
Date of trip
_____

Fahrtgebiet
Area of trip
_____

Reiseroute
Route of trip
_____

_____

Anzahl der Seemeilen
Number of nautical miles
_____

Funktion auf dem Schiff
Position on board
_____

Angaben zum Schiffsführer / personal data of the skipper:

Name
Name
_____

Straße
Street
_____

Plz und Ort
ZIP Code, City
_____

Land
Country
_____

Lizenz des Skippers
License of skipper
_____

Ort, Datum
Location, date
_____

Unterschrift Skipper
Signature skipper
_____

Crew:

_____

_____

_____

_____

_____

_____

Sonstiges / Miscellaneous

Schiffsname
Name of vessel
_____

Schiffsmodell
Model of vessel
_____

☐ Segel / sailing Yacht   ☐ Tide / tidal waters
☐ Motor / power Yacht   ☐ keine Tide / non-tidal waters

Eigner
Owner
_____

Flagge
Flag
_____

Reisedatum
Date of trip
_____

Fahrtgebiet
Area of trip
_____

Reiseroute
Route of trip
_____

_____

Anzahl der Seemeilen
Number of nautical miles
_____

Funktion auf dem Schiff
Position on board
_____

Angaben zum Schiffsführer / personal data of the skipper:

Name
Name
_____

Straße
Street
_____

Plz und Ort
ZIP Code, City
_____

Land
Country
_____

Lizenz des Skippers
License of skipper
_____

Ort, Datum
Location, date
_____

Unterschrift Skipper
Signature skipper
_____

Nr. 22 / No. 22
Kommentare / Comments

Crew:

_____

_____

_____

_____

_____

_____

Sonstiges / Miscellaneous

Schiffsname
Name of vessel

_____

Schiffsmodell
Model of vessel

_____

☐ Segel / sailing Yacht   ☐ Tide / tidal waters
☐ Motor / power Yacht   ☐ keine Tide / non-tidal waters

Eigner
Owner

_____

Flagge
Flag

_____

Reisedatum
Date of trip

_____

Fahrtgebiet
Area of trip

_____

Reiseroute
Route of trip

_____

_____

Anzahl der Seemeilen
Number of nautical miles

_____

Funktion auf dem Schiff
Position on board

_____

Angaben zum Schiffsführer / personal data of the skipper:

Name
Name

_____

Straße
Street

_____

Plz und Ort
ZIP Code, City

_____

Land
Country

_____

Lizenz des Skippers
License of skipper

_____

Ort, Datum
Location, date

_____

Unterschrift Skipper
Signature skipper

_____

Nr. 23 / No. 23
Kommentare / Comments

Crew:

_____

_____

_____

_____

_____

_____

Sonstiges / Miscellaneous

Nr. 23 / No. 23

Schiffsname
Name of vessel
_____

Schiffsmodell
Model of vessel
_____

☐ Segel / sailing Yacht ☐ Tide / tidal waters
☐ Motor / power Yacht ☐ keine Tide / non-tidal waters

Eigner
Owner
_____

Flagge
Flag
_____

Reisedatum
Date of trip
_____

Fahrtgebiet
Area of trip
_____

Reiseroute
Route of trip
_____

_____

Anzahl der Seemeilen
Number of nautical miles
_____

Funktion auf dem Schiff
Position on board
_____

Angaben zum Schiffsführer / personal data of the skipper:

Name
Name
_____

Straße
Street
_____

Plz und Ort
ZIP Code, City
_____

Land
Country
_____

Lizenz des Skippers
License of skipper
_____

Ort, Datum
Location, date
_____

Unterschrift Skipper
Signature skipper
_____

Nr. 24 / No. 24
Kommentare / Comments

Crew:

_____

_____

_____

_____

_____

_____

Sonstiges / Miscellaneous

Schiffsname
Name of vessel _____

Schiffsmodell
Model of vessel _____

☐ Segel / sailing Yacht   ☐ Tide / tidal waters
☐ Motor / power Yacht   ☐ keine Tide / non-tidal waters

Eigner
Owner _____

Flagge
Flag _____

Reisedatum
Date of trip _____

Fahrtgebiet
Area of trip _____

Reiseroute
Route of trip _____

_____

Anzahl der Seemeilen
Number of nautical miles _____

Funktion auf dem Schiff
Position on board _____

Angaben zum Schiffsführer / personal data of the skipper:

Name
Name _____

Straße
Street _____

Plz und Ort
ZIP Code, City _____

Land
Country _____

Lizenz des Skippers
License of skipper _____

Ort, Datum
Location, date _____

Unterschrift Skipper
Signature skipper _____

Crew:

_____

_____

_____

_____

_____

_____

Sonstiges / Miscellaneous

Schiffsname
Name of vessel
_____

Schiffsmodell
Model of vessel
_____

☐ Segel / sailing Yacht   ☐ Tide / tidal waters
☐ Motor / power Yacht   ☐ keine Tide / non-tidal waters

Eigner
Owner
_____

Flagge
Flag
_____

Reisedatum
Date of trip
_____

Fahrtgebiet
Area of trip
_____

Reiseroute
Route of trip
_____

_____

Anzahl der Seemeilen
Number of nautical miles
_____

Funktion auf dem Schiff
Position on board
_____

Angaben zum Schiffsführer / personal data of the skipper:

Name
Name
_____

Straße
Street
_____

Plz und Ort
ZIP Code, City
_____

Land
Country
_____

Lizenz des Skippers
License of skipper
_____

Ort, Datum
Location, date
_____

Unterschrift Skipper
Signature skipper
_____

Crew:

_____

_____

_____

_____

_____

_____

Sonstiges / Miscellaneous

Schiffsname
Name of vessel

Schiffsmodell
Model of vessel

☐ Segel / sailing Yacht   ☐ Tide / tidal waters
☐ Motor / power Yacht   ☐ keine Tide / non-tidal waters

Eigner
Owner

Flagge
Flag

Reisedatum
Date of trip

Fahrtgebiet
Area of trip

Reiseroute
Route of trip

Anzahl der Seemeilen
Number of nautical miles

Funktion auf dem Schiff
Position on board

Angaben zum Schiffsführer / personal data of the skipper:

Name
Name

Straße
Street

Plz und Ort
ZIP Code, City

Land
Country

Lizenz des Skippers
License of skipper

Ort, Datum
Location, date

Unterschrift Skipper
Signature skipper

Crew:

_____

_____

_____

_____

_____

_____

Sonstiges / Miscellaneous

Schiffsname
Name of vessel _____

Schiffsmodell
Model of vessel _____

☐ Segel / sailing Yacht   ☐ Tide / tidal waters
☐ Motor / power Yacht   ☐ keine Tide / non-tidal waters

Eigner
Owner _____

Flagge
Flag _____

Reisedatum
Date of trip _____

Fahrtgebiet
Area of trip _____

Reiseroute
Route of trip _____

_____

Anzahl der Seemeilen
Number of nautical miles _____

Funktion auf dem Schiff
Position on board _____

Angaben zum Schiffsführer / personal data of the skipper:

Name
Name _____

Straße
Street _____

Plz und Ort
ZIP Code, City _____

Land
Country _____

Lizenz des Skippers
License of skipper _____

Ort, Datum
Location, date _____

Unterschrift Skipper
Signature skipper _____

Crew:

_____

_____

_____

_____

_____

_____

Sonstiges / Miscellaneous

Schiffsname
Name of vessel
_____

Schiffsmodell
Model of vessel
_____

☐ Segel / sailing Yacht   ☐ Tide / tidal waters
☐ Motor / power Yacht   ☐ keine Tide / non-tidal waters

Eigner
Owner
_____

Flagge
Flag
_____

Reisedatum
Date of trip
_____

Fahrtgebiet
Area of trip
_____

Reiseroute
Route of trip
_____

_____

Anzahl der Seemeilen
Number of nautical miles
_____

Funktion auf dem Schiff
Position on board
_____

Angaben zum Schiffsführer / personal data of the skipper:

Name
Name
_____

Straße
Street
_____

Plz und Ort
ZIP Code, City
_____

Land
Country
_____

Lizenz des Skippers
License of skipper
_____

Ort, Datum
Location, date
_____

Unterschrift Skipper
Signature skipper
_____

Crew:

_____

_____

_____

_____

_____

_____

Sonstiges / Miscellaneous

Schiffsname
Name of vessel

_____

Schiffsmodell
Model of vessel

_____

☐ Segel / sailing Yacht   ☐ Tide / tidal waters
☐ Motor / power Yacht   ☐ keine Tide / non-tidal waters

Eigner
Owner

_____

Flagge
Flag

_____

Reisedatum
Date of trip

_____

Fahrtgebiet
Area of trip

_____

Reiseroute
Route of trip

_____

_____

Anzahl der Seemeilen
Number of nautical miles

_____

Funktion auf dem Schiff
Position on board

_____

Angaben zum Schiffsführer / personal data of the skipper:

Name
Name

_____

Straße
Street

_____

Plz und Ort
ZIP Code, City

_____

Land
Country

_____

Lizenz des Skippers
License of skipper

_____

Ort, Datum
Location, date

_____

Unterschrift Skipper
Signature skipper

_____

Nr. 30 / No. 30
Kommentare / Comments

Crew:

_____

_____

_____

_____

_____

_____

Sonstiges / Miscellaneous

Schiffsname
Name of vessel
_____

Schiffsmodell
Model of vessel
_____

☐ Segel / sailing Yacht   ☐ Tide / tidal waters
☐ Motor / power Yacht   ☐ keine Tide / non-tidal waters

Eigner
Owner
_____

Flagge
Flag
_____

Reisedatum
Date of trip
_____

Fahrtgebiet
Area of trip
_____

Reiseroute
Route of trip
_____

_____

Anzahl der Seemeilen
Number of nautical miles
_____

Funktion auf dem Schiff
Position on board
_____

Angaben zum Schiffsführer / personal data of the skipper:

Name
Name
_____

Straße
Street
_____

Plz und Ort
ZIP Code, City
_____

Land
Country
_____

Lizenz des Skippers
License of skipper
_____

Ort, Datum
Location, date
_____

Unterschrift Skipper
Signature skipper
_____

Beaufort-Skala

Bft	m/s	kn	km/h	Bez. / Auswirkung
0	< 0,3	1	0	Windstille Spiegelglatte See
1	0,3 – 1,6	1 – 4	1 – 5	Leiser Zug Leichte Kräuselwellen
2	1,6 – 3,4	4 – 7	6 – 11	Leichte Brise Kleine, kurze Wellen, Oberfläche glasig
3	3,4 – 5,5	7 – 11	12 – 19	Schwache Brise Anfänge der Schaumbildung
4	5,5 – 8,0	11 – 16	20 – 28	Mäßige Brise Kleine, länger werdende Wellen, überall Schaumköpfe
5	8,0 – 10,8	16 – 22	29 – 38	Frische Brise Mäßige Wellen von großer Länge, überall Schaumköpfe
6	10,8 – 13,9	22 – 28	39 – 49	Starker Wind Wellen mit brechenden Köpfen, überall Schaumflecken
7	13,9 – 17,2	28 – 34	50 – 61	Steifer Wind Schaum legt sich in Schaumstreifen in die Windrichtung
8	17,2 – 20,8	34 – 41	62 – 74	Stürmischer Wind Hohe Wellenberge, deren Köpfe verweht werden
9	20,8 – 24,5	41 – 48	75 – 88	Sturm Wellen mit verwehter Gischt, Brecher bilden sich
10	24,5 – 28,5	48 – 56	89 – 102	Schwerer Sturm Weiße Flecken, brechende Kämme, schwere Brecher
11	28,5 – 32,7	56 – 64	103 – 117	Orkanartiger Sturm brüllende See, Wasser wird waage- recht weggeweht
12	>32,7	>64	>117	Orkan See weiß, Luft mit Gischt gefüllt, keine Sicht mehr

Beaufort Scale

Bft	m/s	kts	mph	Desc. / Conditions
0	< 0,3	1	1	Calm Flat
1	0,3 – 1,6	1 – 3	1 – 3	Light Air Ripples without crests
2	1,6 – 3,4	4 – 7	3 – 7	Light breeze Small wavelets. Crests of glassy appearance
3	3,4 – 5,5	7 – 11	8 – 12	Gentle breeze Large wavelets. Crests begin to break; scattered whitecaps
4	5,5 – 8,0	11 – 16	13 – 17	Moderate breeze Small waves
5	8,0 – 10,8	16 – 22	18 – 24	Fresh breeze Moderate longer waves, some foam and spray
6	10,8 – 13,9	22 – 28	25 – 30	Strong breeze Large waves with foam crests and some spray
7	13,9 – 17,2	28 – 34	31 – 38	Near Gale, high wind Foam begins to be blown in streaks in wind direction
8	17,2 – 20,8	34 – 41	39 – 46	Fresh gale Breaking crests forming spindrift, streaks of foam
9	20,8 – 24,5	41 – 48	47 – 54	Strong gale High waves with dense foam. Wave crests start to roll over
10	24,5 – 28,5	48 – 56	55 – 63	Whole gale / storm Very high waves, spray reduces visibility
11	28,5 – 32,7	56 – 64	64 – 72	Violent storm Exceptionally high waves, severely reduced visibility
12	>32,7	>64	>72	Hurricane-force Huge waves, greatly reduced visibility

Call Scheme (WRC-07)

	Structure	Example

Distress Alert

Channel	16	16
Keyword	MAYDAY (3x)	Mayday Mayday Mayday
Recipient	-	-
Sender	This is Ship name (3x) call sign MMSI	This is KALINE KALINE KALINE /DETS 211 987 456
Message	MAYDAY (1x) Ship name (1x) call sign MMSI Position Situation	Mayday KALINE /DETS 211 987 456 Position: 54° 42' N - 007° 49' E Explosion on board. Abandoning ship. Need immediate help.
Finish	Over	Over

Acknowledge Distress

Channel	16	16
Keyword	MAYDAY (1x)	Mayday
Recipient	Ship name (3x) call sign	KALINE KALINE KALINE /DETS
Sender	This is Ship name (3x) call sign	This is VIKING VIKING VIKING /DEVX
Message	Received Mayday	Received Mayday

Finish Distress

Channel	16	16
Keyword	MAYDAY (1x)	Mayday
Recipient	ALL STATIONS (3x)	All Stations All Stations All Stations
Sender	This is Ship name (3x) call sign	This is KALINE KALINE KALINE /DETS
Message	time UTC Ship name / call sign MMSI of disable vessel SILENCE FINI	AT 2345 UTC KALINE /DETS 211 987 456 Silence Fini

Call Scheme (WRC-07)

	Structure	**Example**

Demand Silence

Channel	16	16
Recipient	ALL STATIONS (1x)	All Stations
	or ship name or call sign	
Message	SILENCE MAYDAY	Silence Mayday

Retraction of Distress

Channel	16	16
Recipient	ALL STATIONS (3x)	All Stations All Stations All Stations
Sender	This is ship name (3x) call sign MMSI	This is KALINE KALINE KALINE /DETS 211 987 456
Message	Position CANCEL MY DISTRESS ALERT OF DATE/TIME (of distress alert)	Position: 54° 42' N, 007° 49' E Cancel my distress alert of 16th of June, 1405 UTC

Relay Distress

Channel	16	16
Keyword	MAYDAY RELAY (3x)	Mayday Relay Mayday Relay Mayday Relay
Recipient	BREMEN RESCUE (3x)	Bremen Rescue Bremen Rescue Bremen Rescue
Sender	This is Ship name (3x) call sign MMSI	This is VIKING VIKING VIKING /DEVX 211 345 987
Message	AT TIME ON ... FOLLOWING	At 2356 UTC on channel 6
	RECEIVED or OBSERVED ORIGINAL MESSAGE or OBSERVATION	following received: Mayday KALINE / DETS Position: 54° 42' N, 007° 49' E Explosion on board, Abandoning ship, Need immediate help
	END OF MESSAGE This is Ship name (1x) and call sign	End of message This is VIKING /DEVX
Finish	OVER	Over

Call Scheme (WRC-07)

	Structure	Example

Urgency

Channel	16 (or other)	16
Keyword	PAN PAN (3x)	Pan Pan Pan Pan Pan Pan
Recipient	ALL STATIONS (3x) or certain recipient	All Stations All Stations All Stations
Sender	This is Ship name (3x) call sign MMSI	This is KALINE KALINE KALINE /DETS 211 987 456
Message	Message text	Position close to Harlesiel port. Boat out of control. Need tug assistance
Finish	Over	Over

Safety

Channel	16 (or other)	16
Keyword	SECURITÉ (3x)	Securité Securité Securité
Recipient	ALL STATIONS (3x) or certain recipient	All Stations All Stations All Stations
Sender	This is Ship name (3x) call sign MMSI	This is KALINE KALINE KALINE /DETS 211 987 456
Message	Message text	Buoy Accumer Ee unlit
Finish	Over	Over

Call Scheme (WRC-07)

	Structure	Example

Routine (initiation)

	Structure	Example
Channel	16 (or other)	16
Recipient	ALL STATIONS (3x) or certain recipient	Breege Port Breege Port Breege Port
Sender	This is ship name (3x) call sign MMSI	This is KALINE KALINE KALINE /DETS 211 987 456
Message	Message - short	Need mooring for one night
Finish	Over	Over

Routine (further traffic)

Channel	working channel	...
Recipient	Certain recipient	Breege Port
Sender	This is ship name (1x)	This is KALINE
Message	Message text	Arriving with 15 m sailing yacht in approximate 1 hour. Need a mooring with water and electricity for one night
Finish	Over	Over

Einen online Funkspruch-Generator für Ihr Boot, sowie eine Funk-Tafel mit deutschen Erläuterungen finden Sie unter http://www.segel-berichte.de.